This book belongs to

_____

Ninja Life Hacks™

This book is dedicated to my children - Mikey, Kobe, and Jojo.
The truth shall set you free.

Dishonest Ninja

By Mary Nhin

OFFICE

Pictures by
Jelena Stupar

Dishonest Ninja didn't think he was hurting anyone when he chose not to tell the truth.

But what he didn't understand was that each time he lied, he *was* hurting *someone*.

Because when he told a lie, it changed *him* just a little bit each time.

If Dishonest Ninja stretched the truth to impress others, it would never make him feel good enough.

When he didn't tell the truth to get something he wanted, he would worry about getting caught.

And when Dishonest Ninja lied to avoid getting into trouble, he would feel guilty for lying.

But he was forever changed after something happened one day at school...

Dishonest Ninja was playing at recess when he noticed something shiny in the grass. He picked it up and realized it was a watch.

Shy Ninja walked over and said, "Oh! That's mine."
But Dishonest Ninja insisted...

For the rest of the day, Dishonest Ninja's stomach hurt. He couldn't focus. And when it came time for his favorite activity, he couldn't enjoy that either.

That evening, Dishonest Ninja could hardly eat his dinner.

And when his mom asked Dishonest Ninja what was wrong, he responded, "Sometimes, I say things I feel bad about."

His mom replied, "You can always try to correct a wrong. It's never too late."

We all make mistakes.

From that moment on, Dishonest Ninja decided to always tell the truth, no matter what. He liked the way telling the truth made him FEEL.

Being honest helped him feel as carefree as a bird.

Your best weapon against dishonesty is to remember that telling the truth sets you free from worry and guilt.

Please visit us at ninjalifehacks.tv to check out our box sets!

 @marynhin   @GrowGrit
#NinjaLifeHacks

Mary Nhin   Ninja Life Hacks

Ninja Life Hacks